URBAN DOG

Training 2024

Urban Dog Training for Busy Pet Parents

Table of Contents

Chapter 1

Understanding Urban Dog Training the Benefits of Training

One of the primary advantages of urban dog training is ensuring the safety of your four-legged companion. Busy streets, crowded parks, and unpredictable situations can be overwhelming for dogs without proper training. By teaching them essential commands such as "sit," "stay," and "heel," pet owners can have peace of mind knowing that their dogs will listen and respond appropriately in potentially dangerous situations.

Urban dog training also promotes better socialization skills for your furry friend. In a city setting, dogs encounter various people, animals, and stimuli daily. Proper training helps dogs develop the ability to remain calm and composed in these situations, reducing the risk of aggressive or fearful behavior. This, in turn, leads to a more pleasant experience for both the pet and the owner during walks, visits to dog parks, or outings in public spaces.

Well-trained dogs are less likely to cause disturbances or damage property, ensuring a positive and peaceful coexistence with neighbors and fellow city dwellers. Pet owners create a respectful and harmonious environment by investing in urban dog training.

Training a dog in an urban environment comes with its own set of challenges. The bustling streets, loud noises, and crowded spaces can overwhelm dogs and their owners. Let's explore the unique difficulties urban dog owners face and provide practical solutions to help you navigate the complexities of urban dog training in 2024.

Distractions and Environmental Factors:

City life is filled with distractions that make maintaining your dog's focus during training sessions difficult. From honking car horns to sirens blaring, city noise can be overwhelming for dogs.

Other dogs, pedestrians, and fast-moving vehicles can make it challenging for your dog to concentrate. Despite these urban challenges, we will discuss techniques to minimize distractions and create an optimal training environment.

Limited Space for Training:

City dwellings often lack the spacious yards that are ideal for dog training. This limitation can hinder activities such as off-leash exercises and agility training.

We will explore creative ways to effectively utilize limited space, including local parks, community centers, and indoor training facilities. Additionally, we will provide insights into modifying training exercises to suit urban environments without compromising your dog's physical and mental stimulation.

Socialization in Urban Settings:

City dogs need to be well-socialized to thrive in their environment. However, city life's constant hustle and bustle can make it difficult to expose your dog to various stimuli and experiences. We will offer guidance on exposing your dog to urban scenarios, such as crowded streets, public transportation, and outdoor cafes, to help them become well-rounded and confident urban companions.

Overcoming Leash Reactivity:

Leash reactivity is a common issue faced by dog owners, where dogs display aggressive or anxious behavior when on a leash. We will delve into the causes of leash reactivity and provide practical techniques to manage and overcome this behavior. We aim to help you and your dog enjoy stress-free walks in the city while maintaining good leash manners.

Dog training in 2024 brings its own unique set of challenges. You can overcome these obstacles with patience, consistency, and the right strategies and build a strong bond with your urban canine companion. By implementing the techniques discussed here, you will be well-equipped to navigate the complexities of dog training, ensuring a happy and well-behaved dog in any city setting.

The Importance of Training in an Urban Environment

Training your dog is essential regardless of where you live, but it becomes even more crucial when you reside in a bustling urban environment. Whether you are a seasoned pet owner or a beginner in urban dog training in 2024, this information will prove valuable.

Living in a city presents unique challenges for dogs. From navigating crowded streets to encountering various distractions, an untrained dog can easily become overwhelmed or even pose a danger to themselves and others. Training your dog to behave appropriately in an urban environment is paramount.

One of the key reasons to prioritize training in an urban setting is safety. A well-trained dog will walk confidently by your side, obeying your commands amidst the chaos of the city. This ensures they remain out of harm's way, avoiding potential traffic accidents or other hazardous situations. Additionally, a well-trained dog is less likely to engage in aggressive behavior towards other dogs or people, reducing the risk of altercations or legal issues.

Training also fosters a stronger bond between you and your dog. You rely on your dog in an urban environment to be a well-behaved companion. By investing time and effort into training, you are not only teaching your dog essential skills, but you are also building trust and communication. This bond will make your urban adventures more enjoyable and stress-free for both.

The advantage of dog training is ensuring the safety of your four-legged companion. Busy streets, crowded parks, and unpredictable situations can be overwhelming for dogs without proper training. By teaching them essential commands such as "sit," "stay," and "heel," pet owners can have peace of mind knowing that their dogs will listen and respond appropriately in potentially dangerous situations.

Training also promotes better socialization skills for your furry friend. In a city setting, dogs encounter various people, animals, and stimuli daily. Proper exercise helps dogs develop the ability to remain calm and composed in these situations, reducing the risk of aggressive or fearful behavior. This, in turn, leads to a more pleasant experience for both the pet and the owner during walks, visits to dog parks, or outings in public spaces.

Well-trained dogs are less likely to cause disturbances or damage property, ensuring a positive and peaceful coexistence with neighbors and fellow city dwellers. Pet owners create a respectful and harmonious environment by investing in urban dog training.

Chapter 2

Preparing for Urban Dog Training Assessing Your Dog's Needs and Abilities

Understanding your dog's needs and abilities is crucial for successful urban dog training in 2024. As a responsible pet owner, you must ensure your furry friend receives the care, training, and mental stimulation they require to thrive in an urban environment. This subchapter will guide you through assessing your dog's needs and abilities, helping you tailor your training approach to best suit their traits and characteristics.

It is essential to consider your dog's breed or mix and their specific needs. Different breeds have varying exercise requirements, temperaments, and sensitivities. Some breeds may excel in metropolitan environments due to their adaptability, while others may struggle. You can research your dog's breed characteristics to understand their natural tendencies and how they may respond to urban living.

Next, evaluate your dog's energy level and exercise needs. Urban areas often have limited outdoor space, so providing alternative outlets for physical activity is crucial. Assess whether your dog requires long daily walks, interactive play sessions, or mental stimulation through puzzle toys or training exercises. Incorporate these activities into your daily routine to ensure your dog's energy is adequately channeled.

Urban areas can be bustling with people, other dogs, and various stimuli. You can assess your dog's comfort level in social situations and work on gradually exposing them to different environments, people, and animals. Socialization is critical to preventing fear or aggression and ensuring your dog is well-adjusted and confident in urban settings.

Evaluate your dog's training needs and abilities. Assess their obedience, recall, and response to commands. Identify areas where your dog may require additional training or reinforcement and focus on teaching them essential skills for urban living, such as loose-leash walking, proper etiquette around distractions, and good manners in public spaces.

Regular visits to the veterinarian are essential to maintaining their physical health, while mental stimulation and enrichment activities, such as puzzle toys or obedience training, promote their mental well-being.

By thoroughly assessing your dog's needs and abilities, you can tailor your dog training approach to ensure they receive the proper care, stimulation, and training they require to thrive in an urban environment. Remember, every dog is unique, so adapt your training methods to help your dog become a well- mannered companion.

Finding the Right Training Method

When training your dog, finding the proper method is crucial. With the ever- changing dynamics of city life, it's essential to equip both you and your pet with the necessary skills to navigate urban environments. I will guide pet owners

in understanding the different training methods available and help you choose the most suitable one for your urban dog training needs.

Dog training requires a versatile approach that focuses on obedience, socialization, and managing potential challenges specific to city living. Thankfully, there are several effective training techniques to consider.

Positive reinforcement training is a popular method that emphasizes rewarding desired behaviors. You can reinforce positive habits by providing treats, praise, or playtime when your dog follows commands or exhibits good behavior. This method fosters a strong bond between you and your dog, making it ideal for dog training.

Clicker training

This method uses a clicking sound to mark desirable actions, followed by a reward. The clicker becomes a powerful tool to communicate and reinforce desired behaviors effectively.

Clicker training benefits city environments as it helps dogs associate positive experiences with potential stressors, such as crowds or loud noises.

For pet owners who prefer a more traditional approach, obedience training is a valuable option. This method teaches basic commands, such as sit, stay, and come, through consistent repetition and positive reinforcement. Obedience training is a foundational skill for dog training, providing the necessary control and safety measures in busy city settings.

It's important to note that each dog is unique, and what works for one may not work for another. Some dogs respond better to reward-based training, while others require a firmer hand. Understanding your pet's temperament, energy level, and specific needs will help you tailor the training method to suit them best.

Finding a suitable training method is crucial for successful urban dog training. Whether you opt for positive reinforcement, clicker training, or obedience training, the key is consistency, patience, and understanding your dog's individual needs. By investing time and effort into training your dog, you can ensure they are well-prepared to thrive in any environment, making your life together more enjoyable and stress-free.

Setting Realistic Goals for Urban Dog Training

Pet owners must set realistic goals for their furry companions. City environments can present unique challenges for both dogs and their owners, and it is essential to approach training with a practical mindset to ensure success.

One of the first steps in setting realistic goals for dog training is to assess your dog's temperament, breed, and age. Every dog is different, and what works for one may not work for another. Understanding your dog's needs and abilities will help you establish achievable goals tailored to their unique characteristics.

Next, consider the specific challenges that urban environments pose for dog training. In a bustling city filled with distractions, it is crucial to start with basic obedience commands and gradually progress to more complex tasks.

Setting small, achievable goals, such as mastering

"sit" and "stay" commands in a busy park or sidewalk, can boost your dog's confidence and lay the foundation for further training.

It is also crucial to be patient and consistent in your training efforts. Rome wasn't built in a day, nor is a well-trained urban dog. Consistency is vital when reinforcing positive behaviors and discouraging negative ones. Establishing a regular training routine and dedicating time each day to work with your dog will yield better results in the long run.

Remember that training should be a positive and enjoyable experience for you and your dog. Incorporating rewards, praise, and playtime into your training sessions will make them more engaging and encourage your dog's cooperation. Celebrate small victories along the way, as even the tiniest progress is a step towards achieving your ultimate goal.

Please feel free to seek professional guidance if needed. Urban dog training in 2024 may have unique challenges; sometimes, it is best to consult a professional trainer specializing in this niche. They can provide expert advice, tailor training techniques to suit your dog's needs, and help you set realistic goals that align with your dog's abilities.

Setting realistic goals for urban dog training in 2024 is essential for pet owners. Assessing your dog's individual characteristics, understanding the challenges of urban environments, being patient and consistent, and seeking professional guidance when needed will all contribute to successful training. Setting achievable goals and celebrating small victories along the way can ensure a positive and rewarding training experience for you and your furry friend.

Chapter 3

Essential Techniques Basic Commands

Urban Dog Training 2024: A Pet Owner's Handbook," we will delve into the essential commands every urban dog should master. Living in a bustling city environment comes with unique challenges, and pet owners must equip their furry companions with the necessary skills to navigate urban situations safely and confidently.

"Sit" - The command "sit" is a fundamental building block for urban dog training. Teaching your dog to sit on command promotes good manners and helps keep them calm and controlled in busy city streets or crowded areas.

"Stay" - The command "stay" is indispensable for urban situations where you need your dog to remain in one place. Whether waiting at a crosswalk, talking to a neighbor, or enjoying a café outing, a reliable "stay" command ensures your dog's safety and prevents them from darting off unexpectedly.

"Leave it" - Urban environments can be littered with tempting objects, such as discarded food or potentially harmful items. Teaching your dog to "leave it" will prevent them from picking up anything hazardous or unsanitary during your walks.

"Heel" - Walking politely on a leash is essential in crowded urban areas. The command "heel" helps your dog understand that they must walk alongside you without pulling or lunging. A well-trained "heel" command makes your walks enjoyable and stress-free.

"Wait" - When you approach an intersection or need to stop momentarily, the command "wait" becomes invaluable. Teaching your dog to wait patiently ensures safety and allows you to assess the traffic situation before proceeding.

"Come" - Having a reliable recall command, such as "come," is crucial in urban settings.

Whether your dog accidentally slips their leash or wanders too far, a strong recall command lets you quickly return them to your side, avoiding potential dangers.

Consistency, patience, and positive reinforcement are essential to successfully teaching these commands. Dog training emphasizes reward-based methods that strengthen the bond between you and your dog.

Mastering these basic commands will make your dog a well-behaved and confident companion. The skills acquired through this training will enable them to easily navigate city life and ensure their safety in a fast-paced environment.

Leash Training and Loose Leash Walking

Leash training is essential for any pet owner, especially in an urban environment. In the fast- paced world of 2024, having a well-behaved dog that can confidently navigate the city streets is crucial. This subchapter will guide you through leash training and teach you the techniques for achieving loose leash walking with your dog.

The Importance of Leash Training:

Leash training is not just about controlling your dog but also about ensuring their safety and the safety of others. In a bustling city setting, a loose dog can be a hazard to themselves and others, and we are responsible as pet owners to prevent such situations. Leash training is the foundation of a well-behaved dog and will provide you with peace of mind during your walks.

Introducing the Leash:

Start by introducing your dog to the leash calmly and positively. Let dogs sniff and inspect it, associating it with positive experiences such as treats and praise. Gradually, attach the leash to their collar or harness, allowing them to get used to being tethered.

Basic Leash Training Commands:

Teach your dog basic leash commands such as "heel," "sit," and "stay." These commands will establish your role as the leader and help maintain control during walks. Use positive reinforcement techniques, such as treats and praise, to reward your dog for following these commands.

Loose Leash Walking Techniques:

Achieving loose leash walking requires patience and consistency. Start by walking in a quiet, distraction-free area and reward your dog for walking calmly beside you. Use a short leash and maintain a relaxed grip, avoiding tension that might communicate stress to your dog. If your dog starts pulling, stop walking and wait for them to return to your side before resuming. This teaches them that pulling will not get them where they want to go.

Troubleshooting Common Leash Training Challenges:

Leash training can face its fair share of challenges, such as pulling, lunging, or distractions. I will provide practical tips and strategies to overcome these challenges and smooth your leash training journey.

Remember, leash training takes time, patience, and consistency. Investing effort into training your dog to walk on a loose leash will create a stronger bond with your pet and ensure their safety in the urban jungle.

Socialization in Urban Environments

Pet owners must understand the importance of socialization for their dogs in the bustling world of city living. Urban environments present unique challenges and opportunities for our furry companions. Socialization in urban settings and provide practical tips to ensure a well-rounded and socially adept city dog.

Living in a city can expose dogs to loud noises, crowded streets, and unfamiliar faces. Therefore, early socialization becomes essential to help your canine friend with the skills to navigate this urban jungle. As urban dog training techniques evolve, pet owners must stay up-to-date on the latest methods and strategies to foster positive interactions with humans and other animals.

One of the critical elements of socialization in city environments is gradually exposing your dog to different sights, sounds, and situations. Start by introducing your pup to various urban settings, such as parks, cafes, and busy streets, in a controlled manner. This way, your dog can gradually acclimate to the hustle and bustle, ensuring they feel comfortable and confident in such environments.

Exposing your dog to a diverse range of people and animals is essential. City areas are often filled with people from different backgrounds, and teaching your dog to interact positively with strangers is crucial. Furthermore, arranging playdates with other well-socialized urban dogs can help foster healthy relationships and prevent any potential behavioral issues that may arise from inadequate socialization.

Dog training is all about creating a harmonious coexistence between pets and their owners in the ever-evolving urban landscape. By prioritizing socialization, you ensure your dog's well-being and contribute to your community's safety and happiness.

So, as we explore the intricacies of socialization in urban environments and discover how to raise a confident, well-mannered, and socially adept urban dog, let's embrace the challenges and opportunities that city living brings and make the most of our shared urban spaces.

Chapter4

Addressing Common Behavioral Issues in Urban Dogs

Dealing with Aggression Towards People or Other Dogs

Aggression can manifest in several ways, including barking, growling, lunging, or biting. It is crucial to understand that aggression in dogs is often a result of fear, anxiety, or a lack of proper socialization. With the right techniques and consistent training, you can help your dog overcome these issues and become a well-behaved community member.

The first step in addressing aggression is identifying the triggers that provoke your dog's negative behavior. Is it certain types of people, specific situations, or encounters with other dogs? Once you have identified the triggers, you can begin desensitizing and counter- conditioning your dog to them. This involves gradually exposing your dog to the triggers in a controlled and positive manner, rewarding them for calm behavior, and providing a sense of security.

Working with a professional dog trainer specializing in urban dog training can be immensely beneficial. They can assess your dog's behavior, provide personalized training plans, and guide you through the process step by step.

Moreover, these trainers are equipped with the latest techniques and tools, ensuring your dog's training is effective and safe.

Patience and consistency are critical when dealing with aggression issues. Rome wasn't built in a day, nor will your dog's behavioral transformation. Celebrate small victories along the way, and keep going if progress seems slow.

Prioritize the safety of yourself, your dog, and those around you. If you are in a situation where your dog's aggression could lead to harm, it is crucial to use management tools such as a muzzle or a leash with added control. These tools will provide you with peace of mind while you work on modifying your dog's aggressive behavior.

Addressing aggression head-on and providing your urban dog with the necessary training and guidance can create a positive and harmonious living environment for your pet and your community. Together, we can ensure that urban dog training in 2024 is characterized by responsible pet ownership and a safe and enjoyable urban experience.

Overcoming Fear and Anxiety in Urban Settings

Living in an urban environment can be an exciting and vibrant experience for humans and their furry companions. However, it can also present unique challenges for pet owners, particularly when it comes to fear and anxiety in their dogs.

City settings can be overwhelming for dogs due to the constant hustle and bustle, loud noises, and unfamiliar surroundings. This can lead to fear and anxiety, resulting in behaviors such as excessive barking, aggression, or even withdrawal. As pet owners, we must address these issues promptly to ensure our dogs feel safe and comfortable in their urban environment.

It is crucial to understand the root cause of your dog's fear and anxiety. Is it triggered by specific sounds, crowds, or unfamiliar places? Identifying these triggers will enable you to develop a targeted approach to address and desensitize your dog to them gradually. For instance, if your dog is scared of loud noises, you can start by playing recorded sounds at a low volume and gradually increase them over time, rewarding your dog for remaining calm.

Socialization is another crucial aspect of overcoming fear and anxiety in urban settings. Exposing your dog to various people, animals, and environments from an early age will help them become more confident and adaptable. Consider enrolling your dog in obedience classes or urban dog training programs to provide structured socialization opportunities and teach them valuable skills for navigating the cityscape.

Creating a safe space for your dog at home is equally important. Please provide them a cozy den-like area to retreat and feel secure when overwhelmed. This could be a crate or a specific corner of a room equipped with their favorite toys and bedding. Encourage your dog to spend time in their safe space by rewarding them with treats and positive reinforcement.

Implementing calming techniques, such as aromatherapy or music specifically designed for dogs, can help create a serene environment for your furry friend. These techniques can help to reduce anxiety levels and promote relaxation, especially during stressful situations.

Remember, overcoming fear and anxiety in urban settings requires patience, consistency, and understanding. Celebrate small victories and never force your dog into situations that make them uncomfortable. By gradually exposing them to their fears and providing positive reinforcement, you can help your dog become a confident and well-adjusted urban dweller.

City living can be a rewarding experience for pet owners and their dogs, but it may come with its fair share of challenges. By following the strategies outlined in this subchapter, you will be equipped with the tools and knowledge necessary to help your furry friend overcome fear and anxiety in the city.

Managing Excessive Barking and Noise Sensitivity

Living in an urban environment with a dog can be a rewarding experience. However, it has its challenges. One common issue many pet owners face is excessive barking and noise sensitivity in their dogs. In this subchapter, we will explore practical strategies for managing these behaviors and ensuring peaceful coexistence.

Excessive barking can be a nuisance to you as a pet owner and your neighbors. It is essential to understand that dogs bark for various reasons, including boredom, fear, anxiety, or as a means of communication. Identifying the root cause of your dog's excessive barking is the first step towards finding a solution. Once you have determined the underlying cause, you can implement specific training techniques to address the issue.

One effective method is desensitization training. This involves gradually exposing your dog to the triggers that cause them to bark excessively, such as loud noises or unfamiliar people. Start by introducing these stimuli in a controlled environment and reward your dog for remaining calm. Over time, increase the intensity of the stimuli while continuing to reward calm behavior. This gradual approach helps your dog develop a positive association with the triggers, reducing their need to bark excessively.

Providing mental and physical stimulation is crucial in addressing excessive barking. Engage your dog in regular exercise and interactive play sessions to tire them out and prevent boredom. Mental stimulation can be achieved through puzzle toys, obedience training, or scent games, diverting their attention from barking.

In the urban landscape 2024, noise sensitivity can also be a common issue for dogs. Loud traffic, sirens, and construction noises can trigger anxiety and stress in your furry friend. To alleviate their distress, create a safe haven for your dog at home. This can be a designated quiet area with their favorite toys, a comfortable bed, and soothing music or white noise to drown out external sounds.

Consistency and patience are key when managing excessive barking and noise sensitivity.

Every dog is unique, and it may take time to see improvements. Please feel free to seek professional guidance if needed, as a certified dog trainer can provide tailored advice to address your situation.

By implementing these strategies, you can help your dog adapt to the city environment, minimizing excessive barking and noise sensitivity. Building a strong bond with your pet and providing them with the tools they need to navigate their surroundings will lead to a harmonious coexistence for you and your furry companion.

Chapter 5

Navigating Urban Dog-Friendly Laws and Regulations Understanding Leash Laws and Off-Leash Areas

As pet owners living in urban areas, we must familiarize ourselves with leash laws and off-leash areas. These regulations ensure our beloved pets' safety and promote harmonious coexistence within our communities: leash laws, the benefits of off-leash areas, and guidelines for responsible dog ownership in urban settings.

Leash laws are put in place to protect both dogs and humans. They require dogs to be kept on a leash in public spaces like sidewalks, parks, and residential areas. Leashes control our pets,

Preventing them from wandering off, chasing after other animals, or potentially causing harm to themselves or others. Adhering to leash laws reduces the risk of accidents, conflicts, and legal consequences.

City dog training in 2024 has recognized the importance of providing dogs with opportunities for exercise and socialization. This has led to the establishment of designated off-leash areas. Off-leash areas are enclosed spaces where dogs can roam freely and interact with other dogs under the supervision of their owners. These areas are typically found in parks or specially designated zones within the city, offering a safe environment for dogs to run, play, and expend their energy.

Utilizing off-leash areas has numerous benefits for both dogs and their owners. Dogs have the opportunity to engage in physical activities, enhancing their overall health and well-being. They can socialize with other dogs, improving their social skills and reducing behavioral problems. Off-leash areas allow pet owners to meet and connect with like-minded individuals, fostering a sense of community and support.

Specific guidelines should be followed to ensure a positive experience in off- leash areas and be responsible dog owners. Having voice control over our dogs and a solid recall command is crucial.

This enables us to call our dogs back to us in case of emergencies or when it's time to leave. Additionally, cleaning up after our pets is vital to maintaining cleanliness and hygiene.

Leash laws and off-leash areas are crucial for pet owners in urban areas. By adhering to leash laws, we promote safety and prevent potential conflicts. Off- leash regions provide an excellent outlet for dogs to exercise and socialize, enhancing their overall well-being. By following guidelines for responsible dog ownership, we can ensure a positive experience for our pets and ourselves in these designated spaces.

Responsible Waste Management in Urban Areas

As pet owners in city areas, we must maintain a clean and healthy environment for our dogs and the community. Responsible waste management is a crucial aspect of being a responsible pet owner and plays a significant role in creating a sustainable urban environment. In this subchapter, we will explore various strategies and tips for effective waste management in urban areas, specifically tailored to the unique challenges and opportunities of dog training.

One of the most essential practices in responsible waste management is picking up after our dogs. Urban areas often have limited green spaces, so it is necessary to promptly clean up after our pets to prevent unpleasant odors and the spread of diseases. Always carry poop bags when taking your dog for walks, and dispose of the waste in designated bins or waste containers.

Remember, leaving dog waste on the streets or in public areas creates an unsightly mess and can contaminate water sources and harm the environment.

Another crucial aspect of responsible waste management is reducing waste generation.

Using biodegradable poop bags made from plant-based materials instead of traditional plastic bags. These eco-friendly alternatives help minimize the environmental impact of waste disposal. Additionally, you can explore composting options for dog waste, as some urban areas now offer specialized composting facilities or services.

To further promote responsible waste management, actively participate in community initiatives and engage with local organizations focused on urban sustainability. Participate in clean-up drives or volunteer to educate others about the importance of responsible waste management. By actively engaging in these activities, you create a cleaner and greener urban environment for dogs and humans.

Adopting a mindful approach towards waste management by reducing overall consumption. Opt for sustainable pet products, such as toys and accessories made from recycled materials, and choose pet food brands that prioritize eco- friendly packaging and production practices.

Following these responsible waste management practices in urban areas can positively impact our surroundings and help create a better future for our pets and ourselves. Let's work together to foster a clean and sustainable urban environment for dog training.

Licensing and Vaccination Requirements for Urban Dogs

Understand the licensing and vaccination requirements for urban dogs. These regulations ensure the safety and well-being of our beloved furry friends and help maintain a harmonious environment.

Licensing your dog is an essential step in urban dog ownership. It serves as a form of identification and helps authorities locate you in case your dog goes missing. Most cities require dogs to be licensed, and the process is usually simple. You must provide proof of ownership and a current rabies vaccination certificate and pay a nominal fee. Remember to update your dog's license annually to avoid penalties or legal issues.

Vaccinations are crucial for urban dogs as they interact more frequently with other dogs and people. Regular vaccinations protect your dog from contagious diseases and improve your pet's overall health. The most important vaccination for urban dogs is the rabies vaccine, which is not only required by law but also a critical measure to prevent the spread of this deadly disease. Other commonly recommended vaccines include distemper, parvovirus, and canine influenza. Consult your veterinarian to ensure your dog's vaccination schedule is current.

Some cities may have additional vaccination requirements based on prevalent diseases or local regulations. Stay informed about these specific requirements to ensure compliance and the well-being of your dog. Failure to meet these requirements may result in fines or even the removal of your pet from your home.

It is worth noting that licensing and vaccination requirements are not only for the benefit of your dog. They also protect the community at large. By licensing your dog, you fund animal control services and support efforts to manage stray dogs effectively.

On the other hand, vaccinations prevent the spread of diseases to other dogs and humans who may come into contact with your pet.

Licensing and vaccination requirements for urban dogs are vital for the safety, health, and well-being of your pet and the community. By adhering to these regulations, you demonstrate responsible pet ownership and contribute to the overall welfare of urban dog training in 2024. Remember to stay informed about the specific requirements in your city and consult your veterinarian for guidance on your dog's vaccination schedule.

Chapter 6

Urban Dog Sports And Activities
Agility Training For Urban Dogs

Agility training is a fantastic way to stimulate your urban dog physically and mentally. It involves teaching them to navigate various obstacles, such as jumps, tunnels, weave poles, and A-frames, in a controlled and disciplined manner. By engaging in agility training, urban dogs can develop their balance, coordination, speed, and focus, all crucial skills for maneuvering through busy streets and crowded parks.

To start agility training, it is essential first to establish a strong foundation of basic obedience commands. Commands such as "sit," "stay," "come," and "leave it" are fundamental for your dog's safety during agility exercises and everyday urban life. Once your dog understands these commands, you can gradually introduce agility equipment and develop more advanced skills.

When selecting agility equipment for urban dogs, it is crucial to consider the limited space available in urban settings. Opt for compact, portable equipment easily set up in smaller areas, such as collapsible tunnels and adjustable jumps. Additionally, always prioritize safety by ensuring the equipment is sturdy, secure, and dog-friendly.

Patience and positive reinforcement are essential when training your urban dog in agility. Use treats, praise, and playtime as rewards to motivate and encourage your dog during training sessions. Break down each obstacle into smaller steps and gradually increase the difficulty level as your dog progresses. Remember to keep training sessions short and fun to maintain your dog's enthusiasm and motivation.

Agility training benefits your dog's physical and mental well-being and strengthens the bond between you and your furry companion. It allows you to work together, communicate effectively, and build trust.

Canine Nose Work in an Urban Setting

In the bustling world of urban living, finding ways to keep our furry friends engaged and stimulated can be a challenge. Fortunately, there is a fantastic activity that taps into a dog's instincts and provides mental and physical exercise.

Canine Nose Work is a dog sport that mimics the task of working detection dogs, such as those employed by law enforcement agencies. Dogs are trained to search for specific scents and alert their handlers by utilizing their incredible sense of smell. This activity becomes even more intriguing in an urban setting as our furry companions navigate through the city environment's myriad of smells and distractions.

The benefits of Canine Nose Work in a city setting are numerous. Firstly, it provides mental stimulation for our dogs, allowing them to use their natural abilities and engage their brains. This mental exercise is crucial for keeping them balanced and warding off boredom, which can lead to destructive behavior. Secondly, urban Nose Work helps our dogs develop focus and concentration amidst distractions. As they learn to sift through the various scents in a bustling city, they become better at filtering out irrelevant smells and honing in on the target odor.

Canine Nose Work offers dogs and their owners a fantastic opportunity to bond. As a handler, you actively participate in your dog's search, learning to read their body language and cues. This collaborative activity fosters trust and communication between you and your furry companion, strengthening your relationship.

You don't need vast open spaces or elaborate equipment to practice Canine Nose Work in an urban setting. All you require is basic materials, such as scent containers and essential oils, and a willingness to explore your city together.

The possibilities are endless, from searching for hidden scents in parks to navigating through busy streets.

Canine Nose Work in an urban setting offers you and your dog an exciting and fulfilling experience. It taps into their innate abilities, provides mental and physical exercise, and strengthens their bond.

Urban Hiking and Exploring with Your Dog

Urban hiking is an excellent way to exercise your dog's body and mind while exposing them to new sights, sounds, and smells. Before embarking on any urban hiking adventure, it is crucial to ensure that your dog is adequately trained and socialized.

When preparing for urban hikes, consider the unique challenges of the city environment. Your dog should be comfortable walking on pavement, gravel, and stairs. You can use the right equipment, including a well-fitted harness and a sturdy, retractable leash, to ensure your dog's safety during the hike.

Before setting out, research dog-friendly parks, trails, and green spaces in your city. Many urban areas now have dedicated dog parks or designated off-leash areas where your furry friend can romp and play with other dogs. These spaces provide excellent opportunities for socialization and exercise.

During city hikes, be mindful of your dog's energy levels and physical limitations. Start with shorter walks and gradually increase the distance to avoid overexertion. Bring your dog plenty of water and snacks, as urban hikes can be physically demanding.

City exploring is another aspect of dog training that allows you to discover hidden gems in your city. Many metropolitan areas have pet-friendly establishments, such as cafes, restaurants, and shops, where you can bring your dog. Please use these opportunities to expose your dog to different environments and help them become well-rounded and adaptable.

Remember to always clean up after your dog and respect the rules and regulations of public spaces. Being a responsible pet owner, you contribute to maintaining a positive image of urban dog owners and pave the way for future dog-friendly initiatives.

Hiking and exploring with your dog is an excellent way to bond with your furry companion while enjoying the vibrant cityscape. Positive reinforcement and proper training can create a harmonious and fulfilling dog training experience.

Chapter 7

Health and Wellness for Urban Dogs

Exercise and Nutrition for Urban Dogs

Exercise is vital for all dogs, regardless of their living environment. However, urban dogs often need more space and leash laws. Incorporate a variety of activities into their daily routine.

Consider taking your dog on walks, jogging through the city streets, exploring local parks and green spaces, or engaging in indoor interactive play sessions.

Urban Dog Training 2024 offers innovative exercise ideas designed specifically for urban settings, ensuring your dog receives the physical activity needed to thrive.

Proper nutrition is equally essential for urban dogs, as they may have limited access to outdoor spaces for grazing or hunting. Feeding your urban dog a balanced diet that meets their needs is crucial for their overall health and longevity. The book guides people in selecting high-quality commercial dog food or preparing homemade meals catering to their dietary requirements. It emphasizes the importance of a well-balanced diet, including essential nutrients such as proteins, carbohydrates, fats, vitamins, and minerals, to support your dog's energy levels and immune system.

Preventing and Treating Common Urban Dog Health Issues

We must know the common health issues that can affect our furry friends. By understanding these issues and taking proactive measures, we can ensure the well-being of our urban dogs. We will explore the most prevalent health concerns and provide practical advice on prevention and treatment.

One of the primary health issues faced by urban dogs is obesity. Limited space and lack of exercise opportunities can result in weight gain, leading to various health complications.

Prevent obesity. Provide regular exercise, such as daily walks or visits to a nearby dog park.

A balanced and portion-controlled diet is essential.

Another common issue in urban areas is exposure to pollutants and toxins. Busy streets, crowded sidewalks, and polluted air can negatively impact our dogs' health. Walk dogs during less congested times or in areas with less traffic. Regular grooming, including paw cleaning, can help remove any harmful substances they may have picked up during walks.

City dogs are also prone to stress and anxiety due to the fast-paced environment. This can manifest in various ways, such as excessive barking, destructive behavior, or aggression. To alleviate stress, providing mental stimulation through puzzle toys or interactive games can be beneficial.

Additionally, creating a calm and safe space within the home can help dogs relax and unwind.

Cities often have potential hazards, such as broken glass, sharp objects, or toxic plants. Be vigilant during walks and ensure that our dogs are not exposed to these dangers. Regularly inspecting their paws and removing foreign objects prevents injuries and infections.

Proper vaccinations and regular check-ups with a veterinarian are essential for urban dogs. These measures help prevent diseases and ensure early detection of any health issues. It is vital to stay up-to-date with vaccinations, tick and flea treatments, and routine examinations to keep our dogs healthy and protected.

We can effectively address city dogs' common health issues by being proactive and taking preventive measures. Maintaining a healthy lifestyle, providing mental stimulation, avoiding hazards, and ensuring regular veterinary care are all crucial components of a comprehensive health plan for our beloved urban pets.

Mental Stimulation and Enrichment for Urban Dogs

In today's fast-paced environment, it's not uncommon for our canine companions to experience a lack of mental stimulation and enrichment. With the hustle and bustle of city life, urban dogs often miss out on the natural mental challenges and stimuli that their rural counterparts enjoy. However, as pet owners in the year 2024, we have the tools and knowledge to ensure that our urban dogs lead mentally enriched lives.

Mental stimulation is crucial for a dog's overall well-being, as it helps prevent boredom, anxiety, and destructive behavior. By providing your urban dog with regular mental challenges, you can ensure they remain content and engaged.

Here are some tried-and-true techniques to keep your urban dog mentally stimulated and enriched:

Puzzle toys and treat dispensers: Invest in interactive toys that require your dog to work for their treats. These toys engage their problem-solving skills and keep them entertained for hours.

Nose work and scent games: City environments may offer fewer natural smells for dogs to explore, but you can create scent games indoors or in dog-friendly parks. Hide treats or toys and encourage your dog to use their nose to find them.

Training sessions: Daily training sessions reinforce obedience and provide mental stimulation.

Teach your dog new tricks, commands, or even agility exercises to keep their mind sharp.

Interactive playtime: Engage with your urban dog using flirt poles and interactive fetch toys. This not only provides physical exercise but also stimulates their problem-solving abilities.

Enriched walks: Transform your usual walks into opportunities for mental stimulation.

Incorporate obedience training, introduce new routes, and encourage your dog to investigate their surroundings, such as sniffing new scents or encountering novel objects.

Playdates and socialization: Arrange playdates with other dogs or enroll your urban dog in group training classes. Interacting with other dogs provides socialization and mental stimulation through new experiences and challenges.

Remember, mental stimulation and enrichment go hand in hand with physical exercise. A well-rounded urban dog training regimen should include both.

Incorporating these techniques into your routine ensures that your urban dog remains mentally stimulated and enriched, leading to a happier and healthier companion.

Chapter 8

Building a Strong Bond With Your Urban Dog Building Trust and Communication through Training

Effective communication and trust between pet owners and their dogs are essential. Urban Dog Training 2024: A Pet Owner's Handbook guides you in developing a strong bond with your furry companion through training techniques that prioritize trust and effective communication.

Training your dog in a city environment comes with unique challenges. The bustling streets, crowded parks, and constant distractions can make it difficult for your dog to focus and understand your commands. However, building trust and clear communication allows you to navigate these challenges together and create a harmonious dog-owner relationship.

Trust is the cornerstone of any successful training program. Dogs, like humans, thrive in environments where they feel safe and secure. By using positive reinforcement techniques, you can establish trust and reinforce good behavior. This means rewarding your dog when they follow commands or exhibits desired behaviors, such as walking calmly on a leash or sitting patiently at a crosswalk. The more trust you build through positive reinforcement, the more your dog will look to you for guidance and direction.

Effective communication is equally essential in dog training. Dogs are incredibly perceptive and can pick up on verbal and non-verbal cues. As a pet owner, it is crucial to communicate clearly and consistently with your dog. Use simple, concise commands that are easy for your dog to understand. Pair these commands with consistent hand signals or gestures to enhance your communication. This way, even in a noisy urban environment, your dog can understand what you expect from them.

Training should be a positive experience for both you and your dog. Make it fun by incorporating interactive games and activities. Urban environments provide numerous mental and physical stimulation opportunities, such as agility courses or scent work. Engaging in these activities builds trust and communication and helps your dog adapt to the challenges of city living.

Remember, building trust and communication through training is an ongoing process. It requires patience, consistency, and a deep understanding of your dog's needs and personality. Urban Dog Training 2024: A Pet Owner's Handbook is your go-to resource for navigating the unique challenges of urban dog training and fostering a strong bond with your four-legged friend. You can conquer the urban jungle together and enjoy a fulfilling and rewarding relationship.

Strengthening the Human-Dog Relationship in Urban Living

Firstly, it is crucial to recognize that urban living can be overwhelming for our canine companions. The constant hustle and bustle, unfamiliar sounds, and limited space can create stress and anxiety in dogs. We must prioritize their mental and physical well-being to build a strong bond. Regular exercise and mental stimulation are critical. Incorporate daily walks, interactive games, and puzzle toys into your routine to keep your dog engaged and content.

Communication is another vital aspect of strengthening the human-dog relationship. In urban environments, where distractions abound, it becomes even more critical to establish clear and consistent communication with your furry friend. This means using positive reinforcement techniques, such as rewards and praise, to reinforce desired behaviors. Training sessions should be short, focused, and integrated into your daily routine.

Creating a safe and secure environment is equally important. Urban living often exposes dogs to new and potentially dangerous situations. Ensure your home is dog-proofed, with secure fencing and limited access to hazardous areas. Invest in a comfortable, quiet space where your dog can retreat and feel safe when overwhelmed.

Dog owners must be mindful of socialization. Expose your dog to sights, sounds, and experiences from an early age. Enroll them in urban dog training classes or socialization groups to help them develop appropriate behaviors around people and other animals. Proper socialization will strengthen the bond between you and your dog and contribute to a harmonious coexistence in the urban environment.

Prioritize quality time together. City living often means a hectic schedule, but dedicating time to your dog is essential. Engage in activities you and your dog enjoy, such as jogging together, exploring new dog-friendly parks, or attending dog-friendly events in your city. This shared time will deepen your connection and create lasting memories.

Strengthening the human-dog relationship requires dedication, patience, and understanding. Dog owners can build a strong and fulfilling bond with their furry companions by prioritizing their well-being, clear communication, creating a safe environment, providing socialization opportunities, and spending quality time together. Embrace the challenges and rewards of urban dog training, and witness the transformation of your pet into a well-adjusted and happy member of your family.

Incorporating Play and Quality Time into Urban Routines

As pet owners living in city environments, we often find ourselves pressed for time. Between work, social commitments, and the fast-paced nature of urban living, balancing and providing our furry friends with the play and quality time they need can be challenging. However, with a few simple adjustments to our routines, we can ensure that our urban dogs receive the physical and mental stimulation they require.

Play is essential to a dog's life, regardless of their environment. In urban settings, it becomes even more crucial to incorporate playtime into their daily routines. One way to achieve this is by dedicating specific time slots for play each day. Whether it's a game of fetch in the local park or a vigorous round of tug-of-war in the living room, engaging in play with your dog helps strengthen the bond between you and provides them with the necessary exercise.

Prioritize quality time with you and your dog.

Dogs thrive on companionship and attention from their owners, and spending quality time together helps fulfill their emotional needs. Consider taking your dog on regular walks, exploring different neighborhoods, and allowing them to interact with other dogs. This provides mental stimulation and helps them develop social skills, increasing their happiness and well-being.

Urban environments present unique challenges when incorporating play and quality time into our dog's routines. However, there are several creative solutions available. Urban dog parks have become popular gathering spots for pet owners, providing a safe space for both dogs and their owners to socialize and play. Additionally, puzzle toys and treat-dispensing gadgets can keep your dog entertained and mentally stimulated, even when you're not at home.

As city dog owners, it's essential to be proactive in creating opportunities for play and quality time. By incorporating these activities into your routine, you're ensuring your dog's physical and mental well-being and strengthening the bond between you and your dog.

Take a break from the chaos, grab a ball or a favorite toy, and prioritize playtime in your busy schedule. Your dog will thank you for it!

Chapter 9

The future of Urban Dog Training Technological Advances in Urban Dig Training

In recent years, technological advances have revolutionized every aspect of our lives, and the world of dog training is no exception. As city dwellers, we face unique challenges when training our pets. Still, thanks to the cutting-edge innovations of 2024, dog training has become more efficient, effective, and enjoyable than ever before.

One of the most significant technological advances in dog training is the development of intelligent collars. These collars are equipped with GPS tracking, allowing pet owners to monitor their dog's location in real-time. This feature is especially useful in urban areas where dogs can easily get lost or wander into dangerous situations. With the smart collar, you can set up virtual boundaries and receive alerts on your smartphone if your dog strays beyond those boundaries, ensuring their safety at all times.

Another groundbreaking invention in urban dog training is virtual reality (VR) training. VR headsets now allow pet owners to simulate various urban environments, such as busy streets, crowded parks, or noisy cafes. By exposing dogs to these virtual scenarios, owners can gradually desensitize them to the distractions and stimuli they encounter in real-life urban settings.

This immersive training experience helps dogs adapt and behave appropriately in bustling city environments, reducing anxiety and improving their overall behavior.

In communication, technological advancements have given rise to innovative devices that bridge the gap between humans and dogs. For instance, wearable sensors can detect a dog's emotional state by monitoring their heart rate, body temperature, and stress levels. These devices provide valuable insights into your dog's well-being, allowing you to address any emotional or physical issues promptly. In addition, voice recognition technology has been refined to accurately interpret dog vocalizations and translate them into human language, enabling better communication and understanding between pet owners and their urban companions.

Smartphone applications have become indispensable tools for urban dog training. These apps offer many features, including personalized training plans, behavioral tracking, and access to professional trainers through video calls.

With just a few taps on your phone, you can now access a wealth of information and resources to enhance your dog's training experience and strengthen your bond with your furry friend.

Sustainable and Eco-Friendly Approaches in Urban Dog Training

In the rapidly evolving world of urban dog training, pet owners are becoming increasingly aware of the importance of adopting sustainable and eco-friendly approaches. As our cities become more crowded and the environment faces various challenges, it is crucial that we, as responsible pet owners, do our part to minimize our carbon pawprint and create a healthier, greener future for our furry friends.

One of the critical aspects of sustainable urban dog training is the use of positive reinforcement techniques. Positive reinforcement rewards desired behaviors, such as sitting or walking calmly on a leash, rather than punishing unwanted behaviors. This approach is more effective in training and promotes a healthy and trusting relationship between pet owners and their dogs.

By avoiding aversive methods that may cause stress or anxiety, we can ensure a more sustainable and humane approach to training.

Another eco-friendly approach is incorporating environmentally friendly products into our dog training routines. Traditional tools, such as plastic training collars or disposable waste bags, can harm the environment. Instead, pet owners can opt for sustainable alternatives, such as biodegradable waste bags or eco-friendly training collars made from recycled materials. By making these small changes, we can significantly reduce our carbon footprint.

In city areas, space is often limited, making outdoor training challenging. However, there are innovative solutions that can make urban dog training more sustainable. Indoor training facilities with eco-friendly materials, such as recycled rubber flooring or energy-efficient lighting, can provide a safe and environmentally conscious space for training sessions. City dog parks can also be designed with sustainable landscaping, using native plants and rainwater collection systems to minimize water consumption and promote biodiversity.

Dog owners, it is also essential to consider our dogs' diet and waste management. Opting for sustainably sourced dog food made from organic or locally sourced ingredients can reduce the carbon footprint associated with the pet food industry. Additionally, composting dog waste with specialized systems or using biodegradable waste bags can help minimize the environmental impact of our pets' waste.

By embracing sustainable and eco-friendly approaches in urban dog training, pet owners can make a significant difference in their dogs' lives and contribute to a greener future. By using positive reinforcement techniques, choosing environmentally friendly products, utilizing sustainable training spaces, and being mindful of our dogs' diet and waste management, we can ensure that our urban dog training practices are practical and environmentally conscious.

Let's create a harmonious and sustainable urban environment for our beloved furry companions.

Anticipating Urban Dog Training Trends for 2025 and Beyond

Stay ahead of the curve and anticipate the future trends in urban dog training. The world is constantly evolving, and so are the needs of our furry friends in city environments.

Technological Advancements: With the rapid advancement of technology, we can expect to see innovative tools and gadgets that will revolutionize urban dog training. From smart collars that track and analyze behavioral patterns to virtual reality training simulations, technology will enhance training methods and ensure our dogs receive the best possible instruction.

Sustainable Training Practices: As we become more aware of our environmental impact, sustainable training practices will gain prominence. Eco-friendly training tools, organic treats, and responsible waste management during training sessions will become the norm. This shift towards sustainability will benefit our dogs and create a greener urban environment.

Canine Mental Health: The focus on mental health in humans will extend to our canine companions. We can expect a greater emphasis on understanding and addressing the emotional well-being of our dogs. Urban dog training in 2025 and beyond will prioritize techniques that promote mental stimulation, stress reduction, and overall emotional balance for our four-legged friends.

Personalized Training Programs: Every dog is unique, and owners will demand customized training programs that cater to their pet's needs. The future of urban dog training will see a rise in individualized instruction tailored to address behavioral issues, breed-specific traits, and the dog-owner relationship. Training programs will be designed to bring out the best in each dog, ensuring a harmonious coexistence in urban settings.

Community-Based Training: Community engagement must be addressed in urban dog training. In the coming years, we anticipate establishing community-centered training initiatives that bring together dog owners, trainers, and local authorities. These programs will foster a sense of responsibility and encourage positive interactions between dogs and their environment.

By anticipating these potential trends in urban dog training for 2025 and beyond, pet owners can prepare themselves and their dogs for an exciting and challenging future. Embracing technological advancements, sustainable practices, mental health awareness, personalized training, and community engagement will ensure our beloved pets thrive in the urban landscapes they call home. Stay informed, be proactive, and create a positive future for urban dog training.

Chapter 10

Resources for Urban Dog Owners

Local Urban Dog Training Classes and Workshops

Owning a dog comes with its own set of challenges. From navigating crowded sidewalks to dealing with noise pollution, metropolitan pet owners face unique obstacles when training their furry companions. Luckily, there is a solution - local urban dog training classes and workshops.

These specialized classes cater to the needs of pet owners and their dogs, providing them with the skills and techniques necessary to thrive in the urban jungle. Whether you have a rambunctious puppy or an older dog needing some fine-tuning, these classes offer a range of programs tailored to your needs.

One of the key benefits of attending local urban dog training classes is the opportunity to socialize your dog in a controlled environment. In a bustling city, it is essential for your four-legged friend to feel comfortable around other dogs and humans. These classes provide a safe space for your dog to interact with others and learn proper socialization skills, helping to prevent unwanted behaviors such as aggression or anxiety.

Urban dog training classes also focus on teaching your dog to navigate urban obstacles. From mastering leash walking amidst distractions to learning to sit calmly at a crowded café, these classes equip your dog with the skills needed to be a well-behaved and confident urban dweller.

With the guidance of experienced trainers, you will learn practical techniques to address common urban challenges, ensuring you and your dog can enjoy your city adventures together.

Workshops are another valuable resource for urban pet owners. These shorter, intensive sessions focus on specific topics such as recall training, leash manners, or noise sensitivity. By addressing specific challenges, workshops provide targeted solutions for common urban dog training issues, allowing you to make significant progress quickly.

To find local urban dog training classes and workshops, contact your local pet stores, veterinary clinics, or dog parks. They often have connections with reputable trainers and can provide recommendations. Additionally, online resources, such as urban dog training directories or social media groups, can be valuable in finding a suitable class for you and your dog.

Investing in local urban dog training classes and workshops is worthwhile for any urban pet owner. By equipping yourself with the knowledge and skills necessary to navigate urban life with your dog, you will create a harmonious and fulfilling relationship that thrives in the unique challenges of the urban environment.

Recommended Urban Dog Training Books and Websites

Books:

"The Urban Dog Training Handbook" by Sarah Johnson: This comprehensive guide covers all the essentials of urban dog training, including leash manners, socialization in busy environments, and effective communication in urban settings. With practical tips and step-by-step instructions, this book is a must- have for any urban pet owner.

"City Paws: Urban Dog Training for the Modern Canine" by Robert Miller: Focusing on the specific needs of urban dogs, this book offers innovative training methods tailored to the urban environment. From mastering public transportation to dealing with urban distractions,

"Living with Fido in the City: A Guide to Urban Dog Ownership" by Emily Wilson: This user-friendly guide addresses the unique challenges of urban living and provides practical advice for city-dwelling pet owners. Wilson covers all aspects of urban dog ownership, from potty training in small spaces to finding dog-friendly parks.

Websites:

UrbanDogTraining.com: This website offers a wealth of resources for urban dog owners, including articles, training videos, and expert advice. From basic obedience training to advanced urban skills, this site provides valuable guidance for pet owners in urban environments.

CityCanineTraining.com: This website focuses on urban dog training and offers city dwellers online courses and personalized training plans. Their experienced trainers provide tailored solutions for metropolitan pet owners, from puppy training to behavior modification.

TheUrbanPaws.com: This website features a blog with tips and tricks for urban dog training. From crate training in small apartments to dealing with city noises, their articles tackle the unique challenges metropolitan pet owners face.

Utilizing these recommended urban dog training books and websites will equip you with the knowledge and tools to train your dog effectively in an urban environment.

Remember, a well-trained and happy dog is a joy to have in the city, and with the right resources, you can ensure a harmonious coexistence between you and your furry companion.

Urban Dog-Friendly Parks, Cafes, and Establishments

In the bustling city life of 2024, finding spaces where your furry friend can roam freely and socialize with other dogs can be a challenge. However, the urban landscape is rapidly changing to embrace the needs of pet owners with the emergence of dog-friendly parks, cafes, and establishments.

Urban dog-friendly parks are a haven for canines amid concrete jungles. These parks provide designated areas for dogs to run, play, and exercise off-leash, promoting their physical and mental well-being. Equipped with agility equipment, water stations, and waste disposal facilities, these parks ensure a safe and enjoyable environment for dogs of all sizes and breeds. They also serve as meeting points for pet owners, fostering a sense of community, allowing dog enthusiasts to exchange training tips and experiences, and even organizing playdates.

But it's not just parks that are catering to our four-legged friends. Urban dog- friendly cafes and establishments have also gained popularity. These unique establishments offer a space where pet owners can enjoy a cup of coffee or a meal while their furry companions can relax by their side. These cafes often have designated outdoor seating areas with water bowls and even specially crafted dog menus. Not only do these establishments provide a place for pet owners to unwind, but they also create a pet-friendly atmosphere that encourages socialization and bonding between dogs and their owners.

The rise of urban dog-friendly spaces is not only beneficial for pets and their owners but also for the overall urban environment. These spaces help promote responsible pet ownership by providing designated areas for dogs to relieve themselves, reducing the incidence of dog waste specially crafted dog menus. Not only do these establishments provide a place for pet owners to unwind, but they also create a pet-friendly atmosphere that encourages socialization and bonding between dogs and their owners.

As a pet owner in the era of urban dog training in 2024, the availability of dog- friendly parks, cafes, and establishments offers many opportunities to enhance your bond with your furry friend. These spaces provide an outlet for their energy, opportunities for socialization, and a chance for you to connect with like-minded individuals who share your love for dogs. So, take advantage of these urban dog-friendly spaces and create unforgettable memories with your beloved pet in the heart of the city!

Embracing Urban Dog Training in 2024

Urban living poses unique challenges for dog owners. However, with the proper knowledge and techniques, we can successfully navigate these challenges and create a harmonious bond with our four-legged companions.

We have explored the various aspects of urban dog training in 2024 and the importance of embracing this approach. Urban environments present a plethora of distractions, such as busy streets, loud noises, and crowded parks. Therefore, pet owners must adapt their training methods to suit the urban setting.

One of my takeaways from this book is the significance of early socialization. In an urban setting, dogs are exposed to various stimuli, including other dogs, pedestrians, and bikers. By telling our furry friends about these stimuli from an early age, we can help them develop strong social skills and prevent behavioral issues later in life.

Positive reinforcement training techniques. Dog training has evolved to focus on reward-based methods rather than punishment. Dogs thrive when they receive praise and treats for good behavior, and this approach fosters a trusting and loving relationship between pet and owner.

Another crucial aspect of urban dog training is teaching proper leash manners. With limited space and increased foot traffic, dogs must walk calmly on a leash. By employing leash training techniques outlined in this book, pet owners can ensure their dogs are well-behaved and safe while exploring the urban landscape.

Urban Dog Training 2024: A Pet Owner's Handbook has provided pet owners with a comprehensive guide to navigate the unique challenges of urban living. By embracing the techniques and principles outlined in this book, we can ensure the well-being and happiness of our beloved furry companions.

Remember, urban dog training is about training dogs and creating a harmonious and thriving urban community for pets and owners. Let us embrace this approach and make 2024 the year of successful urban dog training!

Acknowledgments

I want to express my heartfelt gratitude to all the pet owners who have shown immense love and dedication towards their furry companions. Your unwavering commitment to providing your urban dogs with the best care and training is inspiring.

Writing "Urban Dog Training 2024: A Pet Owner's Handbook" has been a labor of love and would not have been possible without the support and contributions of numerous individuals. I want to extend my most profound appreciation to the experts and professionals in canine behavior and training who lent their invaluable knowledge and insights to this book. Your expertise has helped shape the content and ensure its accuracy and relevance for urban dog owners in 2024.

I also thank the pet trainers and behaviorists who generously shared their experiences and success stories with urban dog training. Your anecdotes and practical tips have added a personal touch to this handbook, making it more relatable and accessible for pet owners facing the unique challenges of urban living.

Last, I want to express my deepest gratitude to my family, friends, and loved ones who have been by my side throughout this journey. Your unwavering support, encouragement, and understanding have made this book a reality. Your belief in me and my passion for helping pet owners have been a constant source of motivation.

This handbook serves as a valuable resource and guide to all the pet owners who have chosen to embark on the journey of urban dog training. May it empower you to navigate the unique challenges of urban living while nurturing a solid and fulfilling bond with your furry companion.

Once again, thank you to everyone who has contributed to creating "Urban Dog Training 2024: A Pet Owner's Handbook." Your support and collaboration have made this project an advantageous experience.

References

American Kennel Club (AKC) - The AKC is a trusted resource for all things related to dog training.

Their website offers information on various training techniques, obedience classes, and behavior modification strategies.

Association of Professional Dog Trainers (APDT) - The APDT is an organization dedicated to promoting positive, force-free dog training methods. Their website provides a directory of certified dog trainers and articles and resources on effective training techniques.

Urban Dog Training Institute - This specialized institute trains dogs specifically for urban environments. Their website offers online courses, workshops, and resources tailored to the unique challenges of training dogs in urban settings.

"The Power of Positive Dog Training" by Pat Miller - This book is a must-read for any pet owner interested in positive reinforcement training methods. It provides practical advice and tips for teaching basic obedience commands, addressing behavior problems, and building a strong bond with your dog.

"Urban Dog Training: Transform Your City Dog into a Well-Behaved Companion" by Denise Fenzi - In this book, Fenzi provides valuable insights and strategies for training dogs in urban environments. She covers leash walking, socialization, and managing distractions in cities.

"Brain Games for Dogs: Fun Ways to Build a Strong Bond with Your Dog and Provide Mental Stimulation" by Claire Arrowsmith - Mental stimulation is crucial for urban dogs, as they often have limited physical outlets. This book offers a variety of brain games and puzzles to engage your dog's mind and prevent boredom.

"The Other End of the Leash: Why We Do What We Do Around Dogs" by Patricia McConnell -Understanding canine behavior is essential for practical training. In this book, McConnell explores the science behind our interactions with dogs and provides valuable insights into their communication and behavior.

Online communities and forums - Joining online communities or forums dedicated to urban dog training allows pet owners to share experiences, seek advice, and connect with like-minded individuals. Websites like Reddit's r/dogtraining or The Dog Forum provide a platform for discussions and Q&A sessions.

Training your dog is an ongoing process, and staying informed is crucial to ensure a happy and well-behaved pet. These references are invaluable resources for pet owners.